A Wombat's World

written and illustrated by Caroline Arnold

PICTURE WINDOW BOOKS
Minneapolis, Minnesota

Special thanks to our advisers for their expertise:

Peter Courtney, Divisional Curator, Native Fauna
Melbourne Zoo, Parkville, Victoria, Australia

Susan Kesselring, M.A., Literacy Educator
Rosemount–Apple Valley–Eagan (Minnesota) School District

Editor: Christianne Jones
Designer: Hilary Wacholz
Page Production: Michelle Biedscheid
Art Director: Nathan Gassman
The illustrations in this book were created with cut paper.

Picture Window Books
5115 Excelsior Boulevard
Suite 232
Minneapolis, MN 55416
877-845-8392
www.picturewindowbooks.com

Printed in the United States of America.

 All books published by Picture Window Books
are manufactured with paper containing at least
10 percent post-consumer waste.

Library of Congress Cataloging-in-Publication Data
Arnold, Caroline.
A wombat's world / written and illustrated by Caroline Arnold.
p. cm. – (Caroline Arnold's animals)
Includes index.
ISBN-13: 978-1-4048-3986-1 (library binding)
1. Wombats–Australia–Juvenile literature. 2. Parental
behavior in animals–Australia–Juvenile literature. I. Title.
QL737.M39A77 2008
599.2'4–dc22   2007032891

There are three kinds of wombats. This book is about common wombats.

Where they live: Australia

Habitat: cool, wet forests

Food: grasses, roots, bark, and moss

Length: 2.9 to 3.8 feet (90 to 115 centimeters)

Weight: 44 to 77 pounds (20 to 35 kilograms)

Animal class: mammals

Scientific name: *Vombatus ursinus*

Wombats are marsupials. A female marsupial has a special pouch where her baby is carried and fed. A baby marsupial is called a joey. Follow a baby wombat as it grows up in an Australian forest and learn about a wombat's world.

It is nighttime in an Australian forest. A stout, furry animal digs the ground. First she loosens the dirt with her strong front paws and pushes it aside. Then she kicks the dirt behind her with her powerful hind feet. Soon she has made a large mound. This busy animal is a wombat. She is digging a new tunnel for her underground burrow.

Wombats are super diggers. They work like small bulldozers, moving dirt from one place to another.

When morning comes, the air grows warm. The wombat stops digging. She walks down the new tunnel on her short, sturdy legs. She comes to another tunnel. At the end is a cozy room lined with bark. She will spend the day sleeping there. She will stay cool and safe until evening. Then it will be time to go out and look for food.

Tunnels in a wombat burrow are usually about 12 feet (3.7 meters) long, but they can be as long as 100 feet (31 m).

8

Outside of the burrow, she rubs against a big rock. Her body odor rubs off on the rock. Her scent is also in her scat, or body waste. The wombat leaves her scent around her burrow.

A male wombat finds the female wombat by her smell. After they mate, the female chases the male away. In about a month, she will have a baby. She will take care of it by herself.

Wombats have a good sense of smell. They use it to recognize other wombats' territories.

The baby wombat has just been born. He doesn't have any fur and cannot hear or see. He grabs his mother's fur and pulls himself into her warm pouch.

The baby wombat is hungry. He drinks milk inside the pouch. While he is growing in the pouch, his mother eats and sleeps as usual. She takes her tiny baby everywhere she goes.

A newborn wombat is the size of a small bean. It weighs only .04 ounces (1 gram) and is less than 1 inch (2.5 cm) long.

When the forest gets dark, the wombat comes out of her burrow to find food. She uses her strong claws to dig up grasses and roots. She will eat for several hours.

freetail bats

grey-headed
flying fox

brushtail possum

Other hungry animals are looking for food, too.
Small bats are chasing insects. Large bats and
possums are searching for fruit.

Wombats, bats, and possums are nocturnal
animals. They are active mainly at night.

The little wombat grows quickly. At 5 months, his eyes are open. His fur has begun to grow. When he is 7 months old, he is ready to come out of the pouch for the first time.

The baby wombat pushes the opening of the pouch and climbs out. He practices walking. When his mother is ready to leave the burrow, he hops back into the pouch.

The opening of the pouch faces backward, toward the mother's tail. When the mother moves, a strong muscle keeps it tightly closed so the baby doesn't fall out.

dingoes

The young wombat is now big enough to follow his mother as she searches for food. She pulls out blades of grass and lays them on the ground. He nibbles the tender stems.

Dangers to wombats include dingoes, foxes, and eagles.

One night, the wombats hear dingoes howling. *Aroo! Aroo!* These wild dogs sometimes hunt wombats. The wombats run for safety inside their burrow.

After leaving the pouch, a young wombat may still drink milk until it is 15 months old.

The young wombat is now 10 months old. He is about the size of a small dog. He races around his mother, rolls over, jumps, and climbs onto her back.

When he is done playing, his mother uses her long claws to comb the dirt out of his thick fur. Then she cleans her own coat.

The young wombat is now 1 year old. He is too big to fit in his mother's pouch. He has learned how to find grass and other plants to eat.

In a few months, the young wombat will be nearly grown. He will find his own territory and dig his own burrows. He has learned to live on his own.

Where do wombats live?

Common wombats live in the cool, wet forests on the mountain ranges of southeastern and southern Australia and in Tasmania. Southern hairy-nosed wombats live on the dry grassland plains of South Australia and in Western Australia. The northern hairy-nosed wombat is found only in Queensland. It is almost extinct.

Wombat Fun Facts

Long Lives

Wild wombats may live for 15 years. In zoos, wombats have lived as long as 26 years.

Short Tails

A wombat's tail is so short that it is completely hidden by fur.

Comfortable Burrows

Even in the hottest weather, the air in the burrow remains cool and humid. In winter, temperatures in the burrows do not fall below 40 degrees Fahrenheit (4 degrees Celsius).

Strong Teeth

At 6 months, a baby wombat's teeth begin to grow. They are sharp and good for cutting and tearing. A wombat's teeth grow throughout its life. They wear down, but they never wear out.

Fast Runners

Wombats can run as fast as 25 miles (40 kilometers) per hour over short distances. Usually, though, they move slowly.

Big Territories

A common wombat has several burrows scattered over its territory. Its territory can be as large as 60 acres (25 hectares).

Glossary

burrow—*a tunnel in the earth dug by an animal and used as a home*

dingoes—*wild dogs that live in Australia*

flying fox—*large bat with a head that looks like a fox.*

habitat—*the place or natural conditions in which a plant or animal lives*

joey—*a baby marsupial*

mammals—*warm-blooded animals that feed their babies milk*

marsupial—*animal whose babies are carried in a pouch in the mother's body*

mate—*to join in a pair*

nocturnal—*awake or active at night*

possum—*a kind of tree-dwelling marsupial*

predators—*animals that hunt and eat other animals*

scat—*an animal's solid body waste*

To Learn More

More Books to Read

French, Jackie. *Diary of a Wombat*. New York: Clarion Books, 2003.

Morpurgo, Michael. *Wombat Goes Walkabout*. Cambridge, Mass.: Candlewick, 2000.

Sill, Cathryn. *About Marsupials*. Atlanta: Peachtree Publishers, 2006.

On the Web

FactHound offers a safe, fun way to find Web sites related to topics in this book. All of the sites on FactHound have been researched by our staff.

1. Visit *www.facthound.com*

2. Type in this special code: 1404839860

3. Click on the FETCH IT button.

Your trusty FactHound will fetch the best sites for you!

Index

Look for all of the books in the Caroline Arnold's Animals series:

A Kangaroo's World
A Killer Whale's World
A Koala's World
A Panda's World
A Penguin's World
A Platypus' World
A Wombat's World
A Zebra's World